Knitted Dogs

Joy Gammon

Search Press

Introduction

Ever since my childhood dogs have been part of our family. Whether a much-loved mongrel from a dog's home or an equally loved Crufts winner, they have all had a special relationship with us, and knitting their cuddly portraits seemed an obvious thing for me to do.

Knitted dogs have tremendous charm. The choice of breed, size and colour is all yours without difficult decisions such as, 'Is an Afghan quite the thing in our high rise flat?' or 'Can I bear to spend hours grooming an Old English sheepdog every day?' These dogs really do *sit*! They do not moult (well , not much anyway), and they do not eat a great deal, so go ahead and knit as many as you like. If you get overrun they make marvellous presents.

Tools and materials

Needles: exact knitting needle requirements are given in the instructions for each dog. Other requirements are stitch holders, row counters and blunt-ended sewing needles for seaming with wool (tapestry needles).

Yarns: see the individual patterns for exact requirements. The colours are your personal choice. You will need oddments of yarns for embroidering features and paws.

Filling: the dogs are filled with washable man-made fibres. It is worth investing in this as home-made fillings, such as fabric oddments and cut- up stockings or tights, are often heavy and dark in colour and may show through the knitting.

Extras: safety eyes and noses for toys are available in various sizes and colours. All sorts of other extras may be added as the fancy takes you. The miniature poodle, for instance, is wearing a blue 'diamond-studded' collar and a matching ribbon in her hair. A small amount of pink felt, or ribbon, for your dog's tongue, adds instant appeal.

Stitches and abbreviations

Most of the dogs are knitted in stocking stitch (abbreviated to st st), made by knitting and purling alternate rows. The other side is known as reverse stocking stitch (rev st st). Other general abbreviations used in this book are as follows:

alt	alternate(ly)
beg	begin(ning)
cont	continu(e)(ing)
dec	decreas(e)(ing)
DK	double knitting
foll	follow(ing)
gm	gram
inc	increas(e)(ing)
Kg	kilogram
K	knit
K-wise	knitwise
M1	make one by picking up the loop which lies between the needles and knit through the back of the loop to increase a stitch
P	purl
rem	remain(ing)
rep	repeat
tog	together
tbl	through back of loop

The numbers shown in parenthesis, ( ), refer to the larger size.

Sizes and tensions

All the dogs featured in this book are made from three basic patterns: the lying down dog, the sitting dog and the standing dog. Each pattern has two sizes except for the standing dog, which does not work in a larger size. Further size variations are achieved by using thicker or thinner yarns and their appropriate needles.

The patterns are set out in stitch and row numbers so that the proportions will remain correct however much the yarns vary. You, of course, can use the patterns with any yarn you wish at a suitable tension, to achieve the size and colour of dog you desire. If you wish to use the yarns as given in this book, approximate tensions are shown in the individual dog patterns.

Methods and techniques

The three basic patterns: these main patterns and the general finishing instructions for the lying down dog, the sitting dog and the standing dog, are shown at the beginning of each section. Each basic pattern is followed by details of how the individual dog is created, giving the pattern and yarn details required to achieve the final effect. Instructions in the basic patterns are clearly listed in alphabetical sequence so that when you make your chosen pattern variation you can easily refer back to the basic instructions: as an example, the Afghan hound puppy, shown on page 16, is in the lying down position and all the step-by-step instructions are listed under the basic pattern for this model, (see page 14). Only specific details of tools and materials, stitch and feature variations are given in the individual pattern (see page 19).

Making up and finishing: this is vitally important and can make all the difference between success and, at the best, peculiar results, so to help you with the finishing process each basic pattern has its own making up instructions. Always match shapings and ease any fullness in to match before seaming. I usually use back stitch for straight seams, and oversew the finished stuffed pieces together as

invisibly as possible. Tease filling out well and do not over fill because knitting stretches and will distort causing the filling to show.

Finishing touches

As always with knitted toys and portraits, remember to aim for caricature. Be as realistic as possible, but with simplicity rather than fussiness. If possible, work from the real thing, or photographs and drawings, and believe what you see. Poodles really do have ears attached half way down the sides of their heads and dalmatians do have random spots of different sizes. Safety eyes and noses are very successful, realistic and safe. Remember though to be quite sure of where you want to place them before attaching the washer on the back, as they are virtually irremoveable.

Mouths: if you use a dark or black yarn for your dog, a knitted mouth may not be necessary as the seam is an effective mouth mark. But on lighter yarns an embroidered mouth adds character. Dogs' muzzles divide immediately below the nose and, with straight stitches, this line can be added then divided into the characteristic 'Y' shape. Left straight this gives the typical effect of the more aggressive and terrier breeds, (see Fig 1).

A slight curve and extended backwards line gives an impression of charm and friendliness, (see Fig 2), but avoid a teddy bear smirk as this is not a typical doggy expression, (see Fig 3).

Fig 1
embroidered muzzle for assertive breeds

Fig 2
embroidered muzzle for friendly breeds

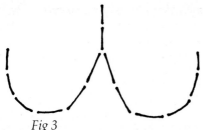

Fig 3
incorrect embroidered muzzle

Felt or ribbon tongues of the correct pink can be added, but need to be attached so that they flop in true canine fashion.

Noses: safety noses are very realistic and successful and, of course, safe. Remember, though, to be quite sure of where you want them before attaching the washer on to the back of the knitting, as they are virtually irremovable.

Eyes: the realistic safety eyes must be placed carefully and accurately. Most of the dogs featured in this book have 'eye make-up' which creates an oval or round shape. Take a line of embroidery from the inner corner over to the outer corner of the eye for the oval-eyed breeds, (see Fig 4a). For round-eyed breeds add a dark 'V' of embroidery at either side of the eye (see Fig 4b), and experiment with lighter colours on the darker coloured or black dogs. A curve of white immediately below the eye gives a soulful look while some breeds and individuals have eyebrows, either marked as tufts or splashes of colour, which can be copied.

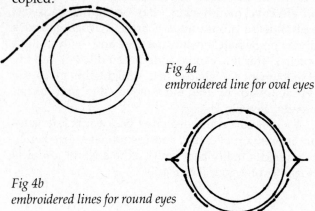

Fig 4a
embroidered line for oval eyes

Fig 4b
embroidered lines for round eyes

Ears: these are important and indicate both character and expression. Ears which flop or turn over always have a fold towards the back, at the attached edge, so that they stand away from the head. Pricked ears are made by curving the base to support the shape and the outer edge is usually vertical.

Claws: if required, these are simply four contrasting straight stitches on each paw.

Markings: spots and head markings can be embroidered afterwards with chain stitch or Swiss darning and can be placed in whatever position suits you and your dog.

Watchpoint:
If the dogs are to be given to small children, remember safety and ensure that all materials used are washable, non-toxic and that all trimmings are very firmly attached. Mohair and angora yarn are unsuitable for very small children.

Knitting yarn quantities and conversions

Most yarns available in the UK are marketed by weight rather than by yardage. The density of dye used to obtain certain colours may result in more or less yarn in each ball, although the composition of yarn is exactly the same. The following conversions are provided as a guide:

25 gm – 0.9 oz
50 gm – 1.8 oz
100 gm – 3.6 oz

Standing dogs

The basic pattern for the standing dogs, with variations, makes the West Highland White terrier, the Jack Russells, the cross-breed terrier and the long haired terrier.

Basic pattern

Main body piece

This is worked in one piece from tail end towards head, with two legs on each side. The work is folded down the middle at the back to make the dog shape.

a) Cast on 78 sts. Work in st st, inc one st at each end of every alt row until there are 86 sts.
Work 2 rows without shaping.

b) Dec one st at each end of every alt row until 78 sts rem. Work 1 row without shaping.

c) Shape back legs. Cast off 10 sts at beg of next 2 rows.

d) Shape body. Work without shaping on rem 58 sts for 40 rows.

e) Shape one front leg and half the head. Cast on 10 sts at beg of next row and work 39 sts, (including the 10 sts cast on).
Put rem sts on a holder.
Turn and complete this side first.

f) Cast on 16 sts at beg of next row, noting that these cast on sts form the beg of the head.
Inc one st at each end of every alt row 4 times.

g) Work 3 rows without shaping.

h) Keeping head edge straight, dec one st on every alt row at the foot edge 4 times, finishing at the foot edge.

i) Shape front leg. Cast off 29 sts at beg of next row, work to end.

j) Shape face. Dec one st at each end of every row 6 times.

k) Cast off 6 sts at beg of next row.
Work 2 rows without shaping.

l) Dec one st at beg of next and every foll alt row until 9 sts rem, then cast off.

m) Pick up sts from holder and work to match, reversing all shapings to complete the other side of the dog.

Main underbody gusset

n) Cast on 3 sts, and work 1 row.
Note: This cast on edge is the front of the gusset.

o) Work in st st inc one st at each end of every alt row until there are 13 sts.

p) Work 20 rows without shaping.

q) Shape inside leg – **Cast on 10 sts at beg of next 2 rows.

r) Inc one st at each end of every alt row 4 times.
Work 2 rows without shaping, (41 sts).

s) Dec one st at each end of every alt row 4 times.

t) Cast off 10 sts at beg of next 2 rows.**

u) Inc one st at each end of every alt row until there are 17 sts.
Work without shaping for 36 rows.

v) Dec one st at each end of every alt row until 13 sts rem.
Work 1 row.

w) Rep from ** to **. (13 sts).

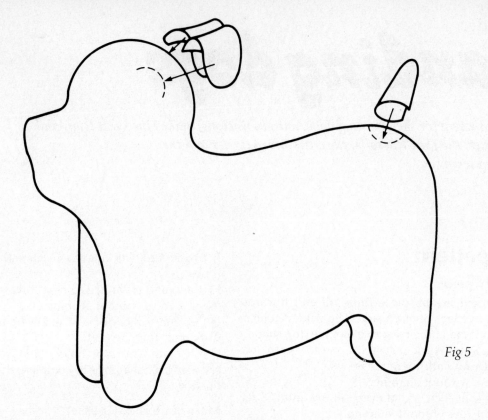

Fig 5

x) Work without shaping for 10 rows.
y) Dec one st at each end of next, then every alt row until 3 sts rem.
Work 3 tog, cast off.

Head gusset

z) Cast on 3 sts and inc one at each end of every 4th row until there are 15 sts.
Work without shaping for 10 rows.
aa) Dec one st at each end of every alt row until 3 sts rem.
Work 3 tog, cast off.

Ears (make 2)

bb) Cast on 16 sts and work 12 rows without shaping.
cc) Shape tip of ears. Dec one st at each end of every row until 4 sts rem. Cast off.

Tail

dd) Cast on 16 sts and work 12 rows without shaping.
ee) Dec one st at each end of every row until 2 sts rem.
Work 2 tog, fasten off.

To make up

To assemble the pieces, (see Fig 5), work as follows: Double main body piece, join top of nose and insert head gusset between back of nose and head division with the wide part, (cast off end), to the front. Insert base gusset, matching legs and easing ends in so that cast on edge joins front of nose and cast off end joins centre of back. Insert safety eyes and nose and fill. Double tail, fill and attach. Attach ears.
Add detail – see finishing instructions on page 3.

Life's a ball!
WEST HIGHLAND WHITE TERRIER

Jack Russell terriers

These two little terriers are happy and playful, although they can be mischievous too (see opposite). Their approximate size is 35.5 cm (14 in) long.

Materials for white Jack Russell

DK, 1 × 50 gm ball in white.
Scraps of brown and black DK.
Approximately 150 gm (5 oz) washable filling.
1 pair medium sized safety dog's eyes and 1 medium safety dog's nose.
Silver yarn.
Silver button.

Tension

24 sts and 32 rows = 10 cm (4in) in st st on 4 mm needles. 4 mm needles are used throughout.

Pattern

Make basic pattern for standing dog in white and st st throughout.
Work 1 ear in brown, altering ears by working 6 rows without shaping at bb), instead of 12.
Cast on the tail in brown and work the first 8 rows in brown, then complete in white.

Materials for brown Jack Russell

DK, 1 × 50 gm ball in brown.
Small quantity of white DK.
Scrap of black DK.
Approximately 150 gm (5 oz) washable filling.
1 pair medium sized safety dog's eyes and 1 medium safety dog's nose.
Silver yarn.
Silver button.

Tension

As given for white Jack Russell

Pattern

Make basic pattern for standing dog in st st in colours as follows:
Main body piece brown.

Main underbody gusset in white.
Head gusset in white.
One ear in black, one ear in white, altering row number at bb), to 6 instead of 12.
Tail – Cast on in black, work 6 rows in black, 2 rows in brown and complete in white.

Special notes: these are happy little dogs so I added curved mouth shapes and expressive eyebrows. The white dog has a large black dot embroidered on his back, and each dog has a crocheted 'chain' in silver yarn and a silver button as a tag. Ears are folded, and tails are vertical, terrier style.

West Highland White terrier

Despite his tough appearance, this dog has a soft heart. I have added a smart traditional tartan collar to make him feel at home, (see page 9). He is approximately 35.5 cm (14 in) long.

Materials

Brushed angora look DK, 2 × 40 gm balls in white.
DK scraps for embroidery.
Approximately 250 gm (9 oz) washable filling.
1 pair medium sized safety dog's eyes and 1 medium safety dog's nose.
Tartan collar.

Tension

22 sts and 28 rows = 10 cm (4 in) in st st on 4 mm needles. 4 mm needles are used throughout.

Canine capers
JACK RUSSELL TERRIERS

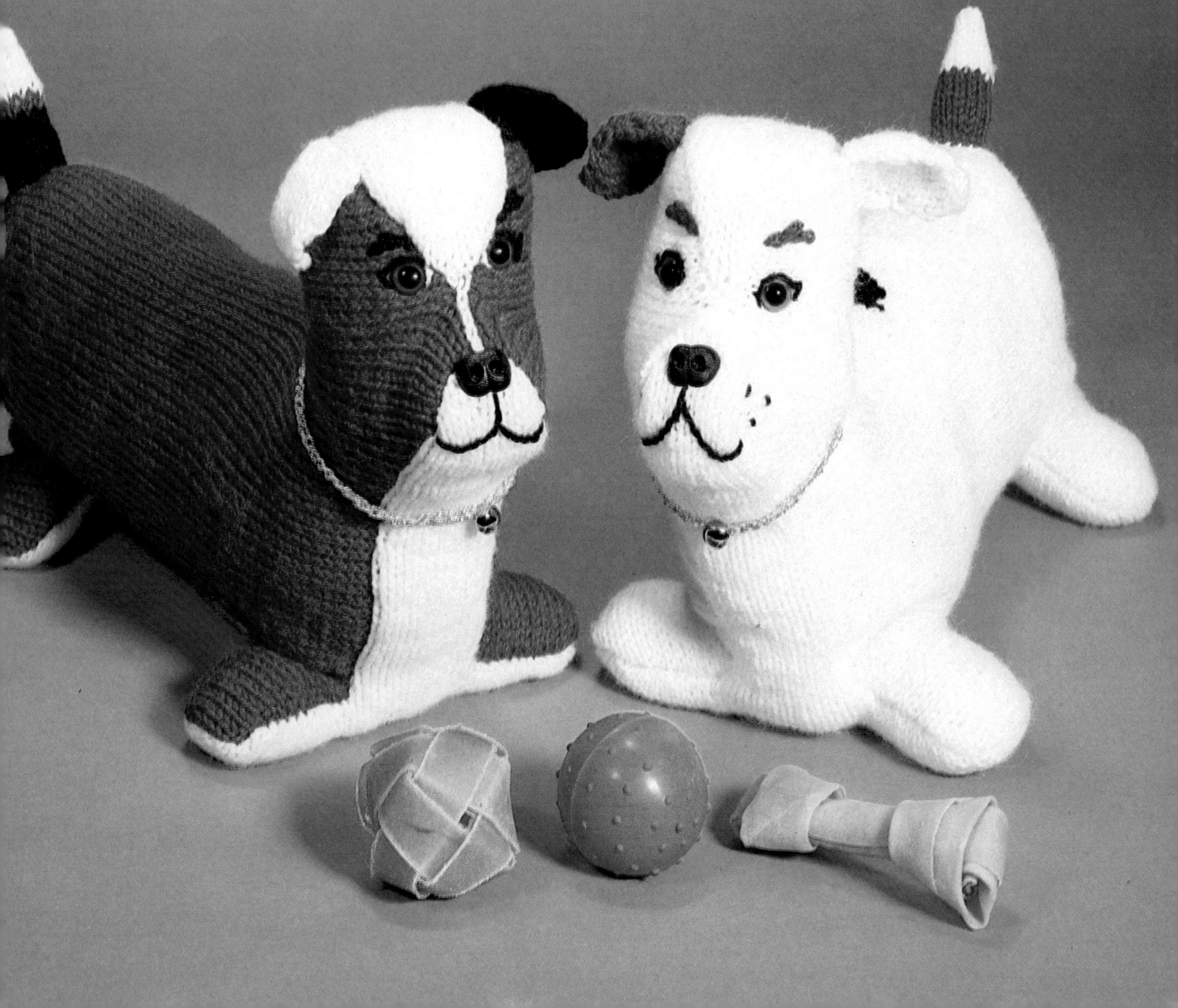

Pattern

Work as for basic pattern for standing dog in reversed st st.

At bb), on the ears, work only 4 rows without shaping, instead of 12.

Special notes: the pieces are brushed on the reversed st st side before making up. Westies have vertical tails and their ears are curved at the bottom, but without a fold, to give a pointed upright effect. They have fluffy eyebrows, with whiskers beneath the eye as well, and they have a tough expression, so do not curve the mouth too high.

Cross breed terrier

This scruffy, loveable dog makes a comforting companion, (see opposite). His approximate size is 35.5 cm (14 in) long.

Materials

Random-dyed DK, 2 × 50 gm balls in brown.
DK scraps for embroidery.
Approximately 250 gm (9 oz) washable filling.
1 pair medium sized safety dog's eyes and 1 medium safety dog's nose.

Tension

22 sts and 28 rows = 10 cm (4 in) in st st on 4 mm needles. 4 mm needles are used throughout.

Pattern

Make the basic pattern for the standing dog in reversed st st.

At bb), on the ears, work only 8 rows without shaping, instead of 12.

Special notes: brush the reversed st st side before making up to give the authentic 'scruffy' look. The ears are folded at the base, but droop, and the eyes have a soulful white line.

Long haired terrier

This terrier can look scruffy unless he is groomed regularly (see page 6). He is approximately 43 cm (17 in) long.

Materials

Mohair, 3 × 50 gm balls in brown.
DK scraps for embroidery.
Approximately 250 gm (9 oz) washable filling.
1 pair medium sized safety dog's eyes and 1 medium safety dog's nose.

Tension

16 sts and 22 rows = 10 cm (4 in) in st st on 5½ mm needles. 5½ mm needles are used throughout.

Pattern

Make the basic pattern for the standing dog in reversed st st.

Special notes: because it is mohair, this yarn can be really well brushed before making up, and 'groomed' afterwards. Attach ears with a pleat, and the tail flat and pointing downwards.

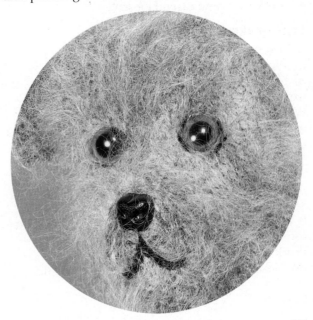

Lying down dogs

The basic pattern for the lying down dogs, with variations, makes the Afghan, the mongrel, the poodle and the chihuahua.

Basic pattern

Main body piece

a) Cast on 21 (31) sts and work 1 row.
b) Next row – Work 1 (3), *M1, work 2, rep from * to end. 31 (45) sts.
c) Work 44 (66) rows without shaping.
d) Next row – Work 1 (3), *work 2 tog, work 1, rep from * to end. 21 (31) sts.
e) Work 1 row and cast off loosely.

Legs (make four)

f) Cast on 15 (23) sts, and begin at top.
g) Work 26 (38) rows without shaping.
h) Shape foot. Next row – Work 1, *work 2 tog, rep from * to end. 8 (12) sts.
Work 1 row.
i) Next row – *Work 2 tog, rep from * to end. 4 (6) sts.
Cast off.

Tail

j) Cast on 11 (15) sts, and begin at top.
k) Work 18 (26) rows without shaping.
l) Shape end of tail. Next row – Work 1, *work 2 tog, rep from * to end. 6 (8) sts.
Work 1 row.
m) Next row – *Work 2 tog, rep from * to end. 3 (4) sts.
Cast off.

Head

n) Cast on 11 (15) sts and work 1 row.
o) Next row – Work 1, *M1, work 1, rep from * to end. 21 (29) sts.
Work 1 row.
Rep the last 2 rows once more. 41 (57) sts.
p) Work 8 (12) rows without shaping.
q) Next row – Work 1, *work 2 tog, rep from * to end. 21 (29) sts.
Work 1 row.
Rep the last 2 rows once more. 11 (15) sts.
Work 1 row.
Cast off.

Nose

r) Cast on 23 (35) sts, beg at face edge.
s) Work 6 (10) rows without shaping.
t) Shape nose. Dec one st at each end of every foll row until 11 (17) sts rem.
Cast off.

Ears (make two)

u) Cast on 7 (9) sts, and beg at head edge.
v) Work 14 (20) rows without shaping.
w) Shape ear tip. Dec one st at each end of next, then the foll alt row. 3 (5) sts.
Cast off.

To make up

To assemble the pieces, (see Fig 6), work as follows.
Fold body piece in half lengthways, so doubling the cast on and cast off ends. Seam one end and the long side seam, (which will be underneath), stuff and close end.

Seam legs and tail into tubes, leaving cast on edge open. Fill and attach legs flat ended beneath body.

Seam and fill head in the same way as for body, inserting safety eyes before filling.

Fold nose centrally, so doubling cast on and cast off edges. Seam cast off and side edge, matching shaping and leaving cast on edge open.

Insert safety nose, fill and attach to front of head. Add ears and detail – see finishing instructions on page 3.

Fig 6

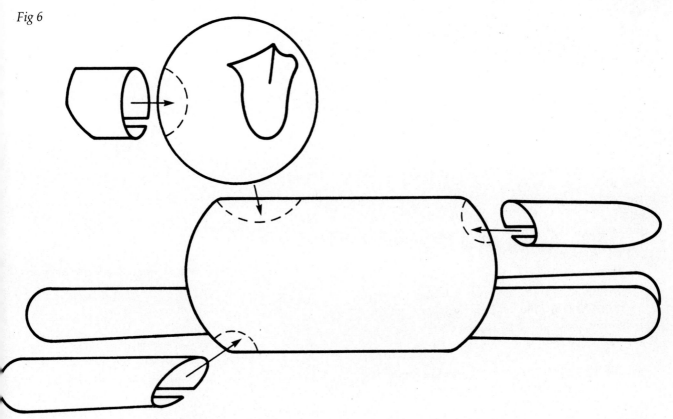

Let me tell you a shaggy dog story
AFGHAN HOUND PUPPY

Give a mongrel dog a bone

Afghan hound puppy

Our Afghan hound puppy is approximately 76 cm (30 in) long, and has been made in a cut fur stitch (see previous page). The loops are cut when work is complete, to give a realistic fur effect. However, the puppy will 'moult' if not handled gently, so if you intend to make this model for a younger child, do not cut the loops as instructed.

Materials

Brushed chunky, 5 × 100 gm balls in pale brown. DK, 1 × 50 gm ball in brown.
DK scraps for embroidery.
About 1 kg (2lb) of washable filling.
1 pair large safety dog's eyes and 1 large safety dog's nose.

Tension

15 sts and 22 rows = 10 cm (4 in) in st st on 5½ mm needles. 5½ mm needles are used throughout.

Pattern

Make the basic pattern for the lying down dog in the larger size but working the nose in DK yarn used double in st st and working the last 8 rows of the legs also in st st in DK yarn used double, i.e. at g) work only 21 (33) rows in fluffy chunky, cont to end in st st in double DK.
Work all of the remainder in fluffy chunky in cut fur st as follows:
Row 1 – (Right side) K.
Row 2 – K1, *insert tip of right hand needle K-wise into next st, wind yarn twice around 3 fingers of left hand, K the st from the left hand needle, K the yarn from around the fingers without removing the fingers, pass the first of these 2 sts over the 2nd, K the next st, remove fingers, rep from * to last 2 sts, K2.
Row 3 – K.
Row 4 – K2 rep from * as given for row 2 to last st, K1.
Work all pieces in this st pattern, keeping it correct throughout all shaping and noting that fur st can variably affect the tension, so ensure that the body piece is roughly square before casting off.

When work is complete, insert scissors into the loops, pull and cut loops centrally, to give fur effect.

Special notes: fur stitch is very stretchy so take care not to overfill. Sewing up fur st is difficult because all the loops get in the way, but the finished effect is well worth it. The ears are attached almost flat at the head sides.

Rough coated mongrel

This dog looked in need of love and affection, so I knitted him a nice, juicy bone (see opposite). He is approximately 51 cm (20 in) long.

Materials

Mohair, 2 × 50 gm balls in brown.
DK scraps for embroidery.
Approximately 250 gm (9oz) washable filling.
1 pair medium sized safety dog's eyes and medium safety dog's nose.

Tension

15 sts and 19 rows = 10 cm (4 in) in st st on 6½ mm needles. 6½ mm needles are used throughout.

Pattern

Make the smaller size of the basic pattern for the lying down dog, in reversed st st throughout.
At v), on the ears, work only 6 (10) rows without shaping.

Special notes: because he is a mongrel, this dog is slightly assymetric with ears attached in different ways, each folded at the base, and he has a soulful look, with white under the eyes. His bone is a rectangle, seamed into a bone shape and filled.

Toy poodle

I added charm to this little poodle by tying a blue bow around her neck (see opposite). She is approximately 33 cm (13 in) long.

Materials

Brushed DK, 1 × 50 gm ball in peach.
DK scraps for embroidery.
Approximately 250 gm (9oz) washable filling.
1 pair medium safety dog's eyes and 1 medium toy safety dog's nose.
Length of ribbon.

Tension

24 sts and 32 rows = 10 cm (4 in) in st st on 4 mm needles. 4 mm needles are used throughout.

Pattern

Make the larger size of the basic pattern for the lying down dog in reversed st st throughout except for the nose which should be made in st st, and the last 8 rows of the legs which should also be in st st, i.e. work 21 (33) rows in reversed st st. Change to st st to complete.
Head – Work as given as far as o).
Before p), work as follows:
Next row – Work 1 *M1, work 2, rep from * to end. 61 (85) sts.
Work 17 rows without shaping at p).
Next row – Work 1 *work 1, work 2 tog, rep from * to end.
Work as given from q).
At k), work only 8 (10) rows without shaping for the tail.
Pom-pon for tail – Cast on 5 sts.
P 1 row.
Next row – In K, inc one st in every st (10) sts.
Rep the last 2 rows (20) sts.
Work 9 rows without shaping.
Next row – K2 tog to end.
P 1 row.
Next row – K2 tog to end.

Run a thread through rem sts and use to seam into a ball, then fill and attach to end of tail.

Special notes: the reversed st st areas are brushed, to give a slightly furry look, and a blue satin ribbon is stitched on around the neck.

Chihuahua

The chihuahua is very simple and quick to make, and he is the smallest of all the dogs featured in this book, (see opposite). He is approximately 17.5 cm (7 in) long.

Materials

DK crepe, 1 × 50 gm ball in white.
DK scraps for embroidery.
Approximately 100 gm (4 oz) washable filling.
1 pair small safety dog's eyes and 1 small safety dog's nose.

Tension

24 sts and 32 rows = 10 cm (4 in) in st st on 4 mm needles. 4 mm needles are used throughout.

Pattern

Make the basic pattern for the lying down dog in the smaller size in st st.
Work only 4 (6) rows at v), for the ears.
Head – Work as given as far as o), then work as follows:
Next row – Work 1, *M1, work 2, rep from * to end.
Work 13 rows without shaping at p).
Next row – Work 1, *work 1, work 2 tog, rep from * to end.
Work as given from q).

Special notes: the ears are placed upright with curved bases and no turn over or fold.

OPPOSITE:
Let sleeping dogs lie
TOY POODLE AND CHIHUAHUA

Sitting dogs

The basic pattern for the seated dogs, with variations, makes the labrador, the poodle, the Old English sheepdog, the dalmatian and the border collie.

Basic pattern

Main body piece

a) Cast on 72 (108) sts.

b) Work 36 (54) rows without shaping.

c) Dec one st at each end of the next, then every foll alt row until 52 (78) sts rem.

d) Dec one st at each end of every foll row until 22 (32) sts rem.

e) Work 1 row and cast off.

Base gusset

f) Cast on 18 (26) sts.

g) Inc one st at each end of every row until there are 24 (36) sts, then every alt row until there are 30 (46) sts.

h) Work 1 row.

i) Dec one st at each end of next, then every alt row until there are 24 (36) sts, then every row until 18 (26) sts rem.

Cast off.

Tail

j) Cast on 20 (32) sts.

k) Work 36 (54) rows without shaping.

l) **Next row – *Work 2 tog, rep from * to end. 10 (16) sts.

Work 1 row.

Rep the last 2 rows once more. 5 (8) sts.

Run a thread through rem sts.**

Back paws (make two)

m) Cast on 20 (32) sts.

n) Work 8 (12) rows without shaping.

o) Work as given for tail from ** to **.

Front paws (make two)

p) Cast on 5 (8) sts.

Work 1 row.

Next row – Inc one st in every st to end. 10 (16) sts.

Work 1 row.

Next row – Inc one st in every st to end. 20 (32) sts.

q) 10 (14) rows without shaping.

r) Work as given for tail from ** to **.

Nose

s) Cast on 30 (46) sts.

t) Work 8 (12) rows without shaping.

u) Dec one st at each end of the next, then every foll row until 16 (26) sts rem.

Cast off.

Ears (make two)

v) Cast on 10 (14) sts.

w) Work 8 (12) rows without shaping.

x) Dec one st at each end of next, then every alt row until 4 (6) sts rem.

Cast off.

To make up

To assemble the pieces, (see Fig 7), work as follows:

Double the main piece and seam, matching shapings and colours if applicable, leaving the base, (cast on edge), open for filling. Insert safety eyes. Insert gusset and fill.
Seam back paws and tail into a tube, leaving the cast on edge open. Fill and attach with straight ends of paws flat under the body, and with tail open ended. Seam front paws into a sphere, fill and attach. Double nose and seam matching shapings, leaving cast on edge unseamed, insert safety nose, fill and attach. Attach ears. Add detail – See finishing instructions on page 3.

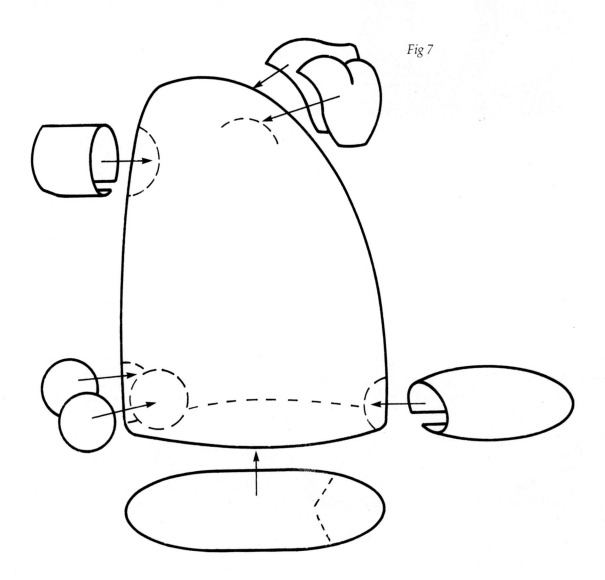

Fig 7

Border collie

The border collie loves doggy yarns and long walks and is looking for a caring owner (see front cover). He is approximately 30.5 cm (12 in) high.

Materials

Brushed DK, 1 × 100 gm ball in white and 1 × 100 gm ball in black.
DK scraps for embroidery.
Approximately 300 gm (11 oz) washable filling.
1 pair large sized safety dog's eyes and 1 large safety dog's nose.
Scrap of pink felt.

Tension

24 sts and 32 rows = 10 cm (4 in) in st st on 4 mm needles. 4 mm needles are used throughout.

Pattern

Make the smaller size of the basic pattern for the seated dog with the following variations:
All four paws in white.
Ears in black.
Tail, cast on and work first 24 (30) rows in black, then complete in white.
Main body piece, cast on in black and work straight rows at b), in black.
Commence shaping, working 8 further black rows

then 16 white rows, then completing the work in black.
Nose, from the cast on edge onwards, throughout the work, work the centre 6 sts in white, the rem in black. Gusset in black.

Special notes: match the characteristic markings when making up, and add an irregular embroidered white stripe between the eyes. I highlighted the inner eye corners with white, and added a pink floppy tongue.

Old English sheepdog

This dog can be brushed to give a fluffy look, although I have given him a smooth coat, (see opposite). He is approximately 46 cm (18 in) high.

Materials

Brushed chunky, 2 × 100 gm balls in white and 1 × 100 gm ball in grey.
DK scraps for embroidery.
Scrap of pink felt.
Approximately 500 gm (1 lb 2 oz) washable filling.
1 pair large sized safety dog's eyes and 1 large safety dog's nose.

Tension

14 sts and 18 rows = 10 cm (4 in) in st st on 6½ mm needles. 6½ mm needles are used throughout.

Pattern

Make smaller size from the basic pattern for the seated dog with the following variations:-
No tail.
Make all four paws, the nose and ears in white.
On the main piece, from the beg onwards, work the centre 16 (24) sts in white, with 28 (42) sts in grey at either side.
When the 36 straight rows at b) are complete, work the shaping as given, *at the same time*, inc the number

Feeling dog-eared
MINIATURE POODLE

of white sts in the centre by one each side on every row until no more sts in grey rem.
Cont and complete in white.
Work gusset in grey.

Special notes: the ears are almost flat on the side of his head and I have added a pink felt floppy tongue.

Miniature poodle

This black poodle has a 'diamond-studded' collar and matching bow, (see opposite). She is approximately 40.5 cm (16 in) high.

Materials

Brushed DK, 3 × 50 gm balls in black.
Approximately 300 gm ((11 oz) washable filling.
1 pair large sized safety dog's eyes and 1 large safety dog's nose.
Dog collar.
Length of ribbon.

Tension

24 sts and 32 rows = 10 cm (4 in) in st st on 4 mm needles. 4 mm needles are used throughout.

Pattern

Work as for the basic pattern for the seated dog, in the larger size with the following variations:
Work main body piece and ears in reversed st st and work 12 (18) rows without shaping at w), instead of 8 (12) rows for the ears.
Work nose and paws in st st.
Work tail in st st working only 8 (12) rows without shaping at k), then cast off.
Work one extra 'front paw' in reversed st st to act as bobble on the end of the tail.

Top knot

Cut a strip of very thin card about 20.5 cm (8 in) long by 10 cm (4 in) wide, depending on the size of top knot you wish your poodle to have. Leaving a short length of yarn free, wind the yarn loosely along the length of card for the required thickness, then leaving an end of about 30.5 cm (12 in) cut the yarn and thread it into a blunt-ended wool needle. Insert the needle through the loops at one card-edge, going under 3 or 4 loops at the same time and bringing the needle up and back over these loops to form a firm back stitch. Continue along the card-length until all the loops are secured (work another row of back stitch if required).

Remove the card from the loops by bending slightly then insert the needle through all the loops at once, but do not pull up too tightly. Now bring one end of the secured loops round in a circle to meet the other end and fasten off securely by tying the first short end of yarn and use the remainder of the yarn to sew the pom-pon on to the poodle's head. Tie a ribbon around the top knot in a pretty bow, and stitch on.

Special notes: brush reversed st st areas, and make up the bobble into a sphere to add to the end of the tail. This dog is such a dense black I added no embroidery, as this would not have shown, but treated her to a smart new collar instead.

Labrador puppy

This loveable little pup is looking for a good home (see page 28). Her approximate size is 25.5 cm (10 in) high.

Materials

DK, 2 × 50 gm balls in cream.
DK scraps for embroidery.
Approximately 200 gm (7 oz) washable filling.
1 pair medium sized safety dog's eyes and 1 medium safety dog's nose.

Tension

24 sts and 32 rows = 10 cm (4 in) in st st on 4 mm needles. 4 mm needles are used throughout.

Pattern

Make the smaller size of the basic pattern for the seated dog, in cream throughout and in st st.

Special notes: the ears have a small fold at the back to give shape. I added typical labrador 'eyebrows'.

Dalmatian puppy

The characteristic spots are simply chain stitched on to give this dog his distinctive dalmatian character, (see opposite). He is approximately 28 cm (11 in) high.

Materials

Crepe DK, 2 × 50 gm balls in white.

DK scraps for embroidery in black.
Approximately 200 gm (7 oz) washable filling.
1 pair medium sized safety dog's eyes and 1 medium safety dog's nose.

Tension

24 sts and 32 rows = 10 cm (4 in) in st st on 4 mm needles. 4 mm needles are used throughout.

Pattern

Make the smaller size of the basic pattern for the seated dog with no variations.

Special notes: This dog is, of course, spotted. I worked the spots in black in chain st though some dalmatians have liver brown spots. These marks vary in size and are evenly spread all over his body. His ears are attached with a fold at the back.

Tailpiece

Making these dogs gave me a great deal of pleasure. I do hope you enjoy just as much as I did creating any of these variations and varieties. Be they mutts or mastiffs, Heinzes or Harlequins, pups or Pulis, – I'm sure that someone will love them dearly.

OPPOSITE:
Puppy love
LABRADOR AND DALMATIAN

Helping hand

If you are a complete beginner at knitting, or your skills are a little rusty, the following information will be helpful.

Place the needle holding the stitches in the left hand and hold the working needle and the yarn in the right hand. Control the yarn by winding it round the fingers of the right hand, (see Fig 8).

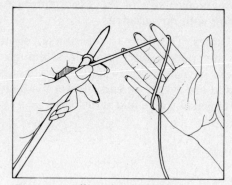

Fig 8 controlling the yarn tension

Casting on

Begin with a slip loop about 15 cm (6 in) from the end of the yarn and tighten it on to the left-hand needle (see Fig 9). Insert the right-hand needle into the front of the loop, left to right, wind the yarn round the right-hand needle point and draw it through to the front (see Figs 10 and 11). Transfer the loop from the right-hand needle to the left-hand needle. Continue in this way, but insert the needle *between* the stitches on the left-hand needle, (see Fig 12), until you have the correct number of stitches.

To knit stitches

Hold the yarn at the back of the work. Insert the right-hand needle into the first stitch on the left-hand needle from front to back, left to right (see Fig 13). This is known as 'knitwise'. Pass the yarn round the right-hand needle point, (see Fig 14) and draw the loop through to the front of the work, (see Fig 15). Slip the stitch off the left-hand needle (see Fig 16). Continue in this way along the row until you have transferred all the stitches to the right-hand needle. Turn the work and hold it in the left hand in preparation for the next row.

To purl stitches

With the yarn at the front of the work, insert the right-hand needle into the front of the first stitch on the left-hand needle from right to left (see Fig 17). This is known as 'purlwise'. Pass the yarn round the right-hand needle point (see Fig 18). Draw the loop through (see Fig 19), then slip the stitch off the left-hand needle (see Fig 20). Continue in this way along the row.

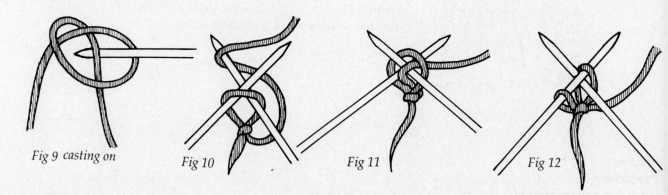

Fig 9 casting on *Fig 10* *Fig 11* *Fig 12*

Knit stitch

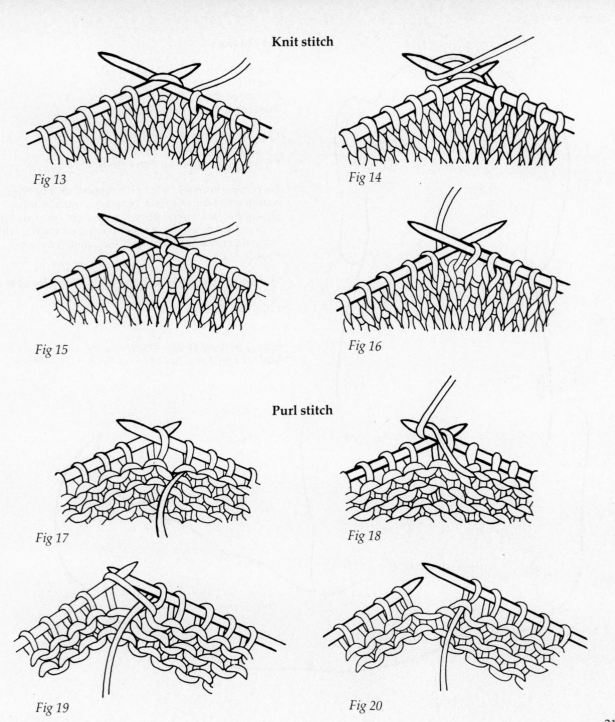

Fig 13

Fig 14

Fig 15

Fig 16

Purl stitch

Fig 17

Fig 18

Fig 19

Fig 20

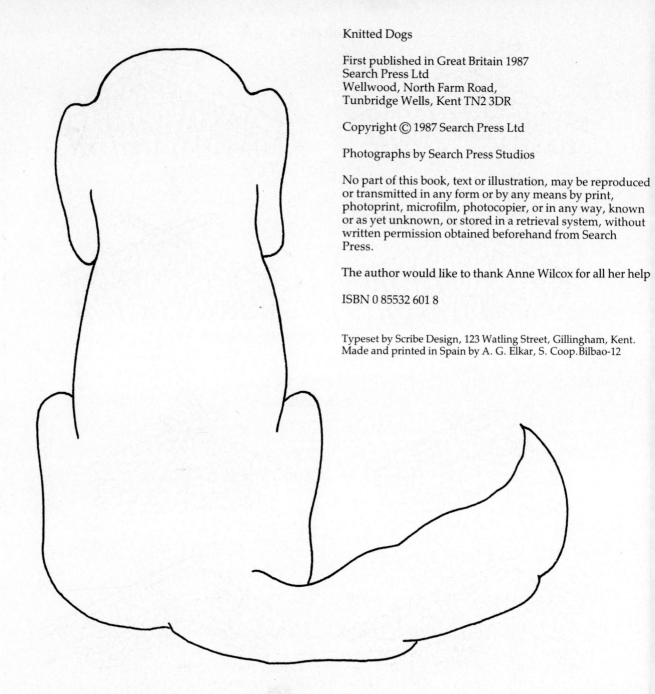

Knitted Dogs

First published in Great Britain 1987
Search Press Ltd
Wellwood, North Farm Road,
Tunbridge Wells, Kent TN2 3DR

Photographs by Search Press Studios

The author would like to thank Anne Wilcox for all her help

ISBN 0 85532 601 8

Typeset by Scribe Design, 123 Watling Street, Gillingham, Kent. Made and printed in Spain by A. G. Elkar, S. Coop.Bilbao-12